Teaching With

Dear Canada

Build Important Social Studies
and Language Skills with Historical Fiction

by
Amy von Heyking

SCHOLASTIC
PROFESSIONAL BOOKS
Scholastic Canada Ltd.

Table of Contents

Teaching Social Studies with Historical Fiction

Historical fiction can be a wonderful way to capture students' interest in the study of the past. It can, however, be used for more than just an introduction to a history unit.

What Can Literature Do for Social Studies Instruction?

1. By including historical fiction in social studies, teachers can provide a greater variety of books for children. This simply makes sense since we know that not all the children in our classrooms are reading at the same level (McGowan and Guzzetti 1991).

2. The teaching of history includes bringing children to an understanding of many complex concepts: change, community, tradition and class, to name a few. Many writers have recognized that stories clarify these concepts for children because they personalize them: they provide a relevant and meaningful context that children can identify with (McGowan and Guzzetti 1991; Van Middendorp and Lee 1994; Brozo and Tomlinson 1986). The authors of historical fiction use language and images evocatively to transport children into different times and places. A 1992 study by Guzzetti, Kowalinski and McGowan demonstrated that sixth-grade students actually learned more social studies concepts and seemed to have a greater understanding of those concepts when they were taught through a literature-based rather than textbook-based approach. Studies have also found that elementary school students' interest in

history and their retention of historical information increased when their history instruction included children's literature (Levstik 1986; VanSledright 1995).

3. Reading stories can heighten children's emotional sensitivity. Their moral and social awareness grows when they consider reasons for people's behaviour in other times, other places or specific situations. Most children have not had sufficient life experience to imagine, let alone identify with, others. Stories provide the "insider's perspective" that allows children to connect with people in other times and places and come to a deeper understanding of others' experiences.

Cautions and Guidelines

Some important cautions or concerns have been raised about the use of historical fiction in social studies instruction.

1. Roberta McKay reminds us that literature is written to tell a story, not to convey information or clarify concepts. Teaching social studies content through literature can distort the purpose of the story. It should not be used as a substitute for the textbook (McKay 1995). When using historical fiction like the Dear Canada diaries, give children a chance to respond aesthetically to the stories they read or listen to. Do not jump into social studies questions or activities without giving children a chance to appreciate and discuss the important literary elements of the diaries. Talk about the way the authors used language in the diaries. How does the

language or vocabulary the authors used make it seem as if they really were written long ago? Make a glossary of all the unusual or new words. How did they evoke a sense of the past? What were the important turning points in the diary? How did the authors make you want to keep reading? Did you get a real sense of place in the description of the setting? Discuss the characters in the diaries. Would you like to meet the fictional writer of the diary? Would she be a good friend?

2. It is vital that even the youngest students begin to distinguish between factual and fictional writing. Integrating fictional stories into lessons in a content area (which is usually factual) can confuse them if explicit instruction in the two kinds of writing is not given. Teachers must teach the distinction between fiction and non-fiction literature explicitly, directly and often. Indeed, Levstik and Barton suggest that historical narratives carry extraordinary authority for children, and reading them to begin a unit may actually undermine children's attempts to do research on the topic or approach their research in an objective way. It takes careful, deliberate and teacher-directed work with fiction and non-fiction text to help children understand the complex "truth" of an historical episode (2001). Reading a range of fiction and non-fiction books on the same subject will help children examine various books critically, determining the interpretation the authors present. Levstik (1993) tells us that children, "need to be exposed not just to textbooks and historical fiction, but also to biographies, autobiographies, informational texts, and even oral history; they need to be able to distinguish the features of each

form and to recognize their strengths and limitations. They will then learn to ask who is telling the story and to whom, and who is left out." Consider asking students how the authors of the Dear Canada diaries make their characters seem like "real" people. As students are reading, continually ask them how the author might have known specific historical details. (For example: How would Carol Matas have found out what Cree women did with buffalo? How did Sarah Ellis know what games children played in the 1920s?) After reading the diaries and doing research on the historical period, ask them to identify elements in the diary that are obvious fiction. Use a Venn diagram to compare and contrast the diary with a non-fiction book on the same historical period. Place all the books students consulted on a continuum from "completely fictional" to "completely factual" and ask them to defend the way they placed the books.

3. Using historical fiction can obscure the fact that the past is a different place. While it can be important to motivate students' interest in the past, historical fiction can distort history and the experience of people in the past when it pretends that they were just like us. Anne Scott MacLeod reminds us that "people of the past were not just us in odd clothing. They were people who saw the world differently; approached human relationships differently; people for whom night and day, heat and cold, seasons and work and play had meanings lost to an industrialized world." (Quoted in Edinger 2000, 124.) There is a concern that we are actually encouraging a dangerous "presentism" or "present-mindedness" in children when we emphasize the similarities between the past

and present and suggest to children that they are even capable of understanding the experience of people in the past through the reading of historical fiction. Remember to ask students critical questions about the Dear Canada diaries when you are reading them: Why are real diaries written by children so difficult to find? Is it realistic to imagine girls like these keeping diaries? Why are all the fictional writers of the diaries a little bit eccentric? In what ways are the girls written to appeal to modern readers?

These cautions and guidelines are intended not to discourage teachers from using historical fiction, but are simply a reminder that it should be used judiciously and appropriately. At its most powerful, historical fiction becomes a springboard for students' own questions about the past.

Activities for General Use

Three activities that can be applied to any of the Dear Canada books are available on pages 45 to 47. (Activities and reproducibles for use with specific titles are included within each title's section.)

Bibliography

Brophy, Jere and VanSledright, Bruce. (1997). *Teaching and Learning History in Elementary Schools.* New York: Teachers College Press.

Brozo, W.G. and Tomlinson, C.M. (1986). "Literature: The Key to Lively Content Courses." *The Reading Teacher,* 40, 3: 288–93.

Davis, John C., III and Palmer, Jesse. (1992). "A Strategy for Using Children's Literature to Extend the Social Studies Curriculum." *The Social Studies,* 83, 3: 125–128.

Edinger, Monica. (2000). *Seeking History: Teaching with Primary Sources in Grades 4–6.* Portsmouth, N.H.: Heinemann.

Guzzetti, B., Kowalinksi, B. and McGowan, T. (1992). "Using a Literature-Based Approach to Teaching Social Studies." *Journal of Reading,* 36: 114–22.

Jorgensen, Karen L. (1993). *History Workshop: Reconstructing the Past with Elementary Students.* Portsmouth, N.H.: Heinemann.

Levstik, Linda S. (1993). "Making the Past Come to Life." In Bernice E. Cullinan (Ed.), *Fact and Fiction: Literature Across the Curriculum* (pp. 5–13). Newark, Del.: International Reading Association.

Levstik, Linda S. (1986). "The Relationship Between Historical Response and Narrative in a Sixth Grade Classroom." *Theory and Research in Social Education,* 14: 1–19.

Levstik, Linda S. and Barton, Keith C. (2001). *Doing History,* 2nd ed. Mahwah, N.J.: Lawrence Erlbaum Associates.

McGowan, T. and Guzzetti, B. (1991). "Promoting Social Studies Understanding Through Literature-Based Instruction." *The Social Studies,* 82, 1: 16–21.

McKay, Roberta. (1997). "Promoting the Aesthetic Experience: Responding to Literature in Social Studies." In Roland Case and Penney Clark (Eds.), *The Canadian Anthology of Social Studies* (pp. 349–360). Vancouver: Pacific Educational Press.

McKay, Roberta. (1995). "Using Literature in Social Studies: A Caution." *Canadian Social Studies,* 29 (3): 95–6.

A Timeline of Canadian History

About 18000 B.C. — The first inhabitants of North America probably cross from Siberia via a land bridge.

About A.D. 1001 — Leif Ericsson makes his first voyage to Vinland.

1497 — John Cabot makes the first of two voyages for England to the fishing grounds of Newfoundland.

1534 — Jacques Cartier claims the Gaspé peninsula for France. The following year he travels up the St. Lawrence to Stadacona and Hochelaga and names the territory "Canada."

1576 — Martin Frobisher makes the first of three journeys to find the Northwest Passage.

1583 — Sir Humphrey Gilbert claims Newfoundland for England.

1604 — Samuel de Champlain establishes a colony at Nova Scotia.

1608 — Champlain establishes a permanent French colony at Québec.

1615 — The first Roman Catholic missionaries attempt to convert aboriginal people to Christianity.

1642 — The founding of Montreal.

1649 — The Iroquois complete the destruction of the Huron nation and begin to raid French settlements.

1663 — Jean Talon is appointed Intendant of New France. King Louis XIV commits to defending the colony and promoting settlement.

1670 — The British crown grants a charter to the Hudson's Bay Company.

1713 — The Treaty of Utrecht.

1749 — The British establish Halifax.

1755 — The British begin the expulsion of the Acadians.

1756–1763 — The Seven Years War between Britain and France, during which the British capture Louisbourg (1758), capture Québec in the battle of the Plains of Abraham (1759), and the French surrender New France to the British (1760).

1769 — Prince Edward Island becomes a colony of Great Britain.

1774 — The passage of the Québec Act.

1776 — The creation of the North West Company.

1778 — Captain James Cook explores the Pacific Coast.

1775–1783 — The American Revolutionary War, during which the Thirteen Colonies gain independence from Great Britain. The people of Québec, Nova Scotia and Prince Edward Island remain loyal to Great Britain. About forty thousand Loyalists from the Thirteen Colonies join them.

1783–1784   ***With Nothing But Our Courage***

1791   Québec is divided into two separate colonies: Lower and Upper Canada.

1792   Captain George Vancouver makes the first of three voyages to explore Vancouver Island and the coast of British Columbia.

1793   Explorer Alexander Mackenzie crosses the Rocky and Coastal Mountains to reach the Pacific Ocean.

1793   John Graves Simcoe establishes York (now Toronto) on the shore of Lake Ontario.

1811   The first group of Lord Selkirk's settlers arrives at Hudson Bay.

1812–1815   The War of 1812, between Great Britain and the United States, in which Isaac Brock is killed (Battle of Queenston Heights in 1812), Laura Secord becomes a hero (1813), and Tecumseh dies (1813).

1815–1817   ***Footsteps in the Snow***

1837   Rebellions in Upper and Lower Canada result in a visit from Lord Durham and the recommendation that the colonies should receive responsible government.

1841   The Act of Union unites Upper and Lower Canada into the Province of Canada.

1843   Victoria is established on Vancouver Island.

1851   Canada's first postage stamp is issued. It has only been possible to send mail overseas for about ten years.

1857   Ottawa becomes the new capital of Canada.

1858   British Columbia becomes a colony of Great Britain when gold is discovered in the Fraser River.

1867   The British North America Act is passed. New Brunswick, Nova Scotia, Québec and Ontario form the Dominion of Canada.

1869   The Métis in the Red River region rebel when Canada purchases the territory from the Hudson's Bay Company.

1870   The province of Manitoba joins Confederation. The Northwest Territories are created.

1871   British Columbia joins Confederation.

1873   The Cypress Hills massacre results in the creation of the North West Mounted Police to keep order in the new territories.

1873   Prince Edward Island joins Confederation.

1885   The Métis of the Northwest Territories rebel against the Canadian government. Their leader, Louis Riel, is later hanged.

1885   The last spike of the main line of the Canadian Pacific Railway is driven at Craigellachie, British Columbia.

1896	Gold is discovered in the Klondike.
1897	***Orphan at My Door***
1898	Yukon becomes a federal territory.
1899–1902	Canadians fight for the British during the Boer War in South Africa.
1905	Saskatchewan and Alberta join Confederation.
1914–1918	Britain declares war on Germany. Canada participates as part of the British Empire.
1917	The Halifax explosion.
1918	Women are granted the right to vote in federal elections.
1919	The Winnipeg general strike.
1926–1927	***A Prairie as Wide as the Sea***
1927	The first coast-to-coast radio broadcast in Canada.
1929	The Persons Case.
1929	The stock market crash of October 29 marks the beginning of the Great Depression.
1936	The establishment of the Canadian Broadcasting Corporation.
1939–45	Canada participates in the Second World War.
1947	The oil strike at Leduc No. 1 in Alberta marks the beginning of the province's oil boom.
1949	Newfoundland joins Confederation.
1960	Aboriginal people living on reserves are granted the right to vote in federal elections.
1965	Canada adopts a new flag featuring a red maple leaf.
1970	The FLQ, a terrorist group attempting to establish an independent Québec through revolution, kidnaps a British trade commissioner and a Québec cabinet minister. The federal government, under Prime Minister Pierre Trudeau, invokes the War Measures Act.
1982	The Constitution Act is passed, along with the Canadian Charter of Rights and Freedoms.
1989	The North American Free Trade Agreement comes into effect.
1999	Nunavut becomes a federal territory.

With Nothing But Our Courage

The Loyalist Diary of Mary MacDonald

Johnstown, Québec, 1783

Summary: Mary MacDonald, her parents, grandmother and younger siblings must flee their home in Albany County, New York, because they have been loyal to the British Crown through the American War of Independence. Now that it is clear that the American rebels (called Patriots) have won, they are no longer safe or welcome in their home. They undertake a dangerous overland journey, north along the Hudson River, over Lake Champlain, and north along the Richelieu River to Sorel, Québec. There they are reunited with Mary's older brother Angus who has been fighting for the King's Royal Regiment of New York. During their dangerous journey they lose virtually all their possessions, but they gain Mohawk friends and learn about living off the land. Eventually they take possession of new land at Johnstown, Québec, and begin to make a new life as Canadians.

What's Going On in the World in 1783?

- Thousands of Loyalists flee to Nova Scotia, where they are granted free land and supplies. Black Loyalists are granted smaller land allotments, fewer rations and inadequate tools.

- Spain has recently completed its conquest of Florida.

- Warren Hastings is busy conquering India for the British.

- James Watt just invented the rotary steam engine.

- Beethoven's first works are printed; Mozart's Mass in C Minor premieres.

- "Enlightenment" philosophers Kant and Rousseau publish major works.

Prior Knowledge

Ask students to define the term "refugee." Identify groups of people who have come as recent refugees to Canada (from Bosnia, Sierra Leone, Vietnam, etc.). Discuss their reasons for fleeing their countries to come to Canada — war, danger, human rights abuses. Keep a chart with this information handy while reading Mary MacDonald's diary, so you can draw students' attention to the similarities in the conditions facing the MacDonalds and the conditions facing recent refugees. Discuss the roots of the conflict between the British and the American colonists that culminated in the American Revolutionary War. Point out that while many regions within the Thirteen Colonies tended to either support or reject the rebels, in many cases communities and even families were divided in their loyalties. (In this sense this war was really a "civil" war.) Define terms students will need to understand to make sense of the diary, such as Patriot, rebel, Loyalist and Tory.

Discussion Questions

Fleeing Albany (October 6, 1783 to October 10, 1783)

✍ Mary's father is humiliated by his neighbours (pp. 4–6). Find out about other treatments Loyalists received at the hands of their neighbours, such as tarring and feathering, and riding the rail.

✍ The War of Independence began in 1776. Is it likely that Mary's neighbours only "turned on" them in 1783?

✍ List the items that the MacDonald family took with them when they fled their home (p. 7). Why do you think the diary is called *With Nothing But Our Courage*, if they took all of these household items? What would you take if you were forced to leave your house in 24 hours?

✍ Why is the lilac bush so important to Grannie? What does it symbolize?

✍ Mary says that it is important to write things down (p. 12). What do you think this means? Do you think the "writing down of things" is important?

Along the Hudson River Valley (October 11, 1783 to November 1, 1783)

✍ Why do you think Mary's mother is so depressed (p. 19)?

✍ Make a sketch of a typical campsite that the MacDonalds created in the course of their journey (p. 22).

❧ Why doesn't Grannie think they should travel on Sundays (p. 23)? Find out more about Presbyterians.

❧ Why is Mary so frightened by the Indian who appears at the campsite (p. 27)? Why is her father so pleased to join the Mohawks on the trail?

❧ Mary describes some of the sights, sounds and smells of the journey (pp. 30–33). Create a "five senses cluster" to describe her journey.

❧ The MacDonalds part from their Mohawk friend John at the Mettawee (p. 38). Review all the things that John did for the MacDonalds, and write a thank-you note Mr. MacDonald might have written to him if he'd had the time.

Loyalist pioneers crossing
the stream, Ontario

❧ Mary writes that her father's mind seems to be "all closed off" (p. 40). Describe what you think is going on in the minds of Mary's father, mother and grandmother at this point in their journey.

❧ On October 24 the MacDonalds reach Chimney Point (p. 42). Check a map and identify which mountains Mary sees.

❧ When the MacDonalds discover that they will not be able to take their possessions to Québec, Mrs. MacDonald insists that she take her good china platter (p. 47). Why do you think this is so important to her?

❧ On Lake Champlain the MacDonalds travel with a family that owns slaves (pp. 52–53). What do you think will happen to these slaves once they reach Québec?

❧ Compare and contrast the attitudes of Mrs. MacDonald and Mrs. Ross on the journey. Why do you think they face their trials so differently?

In Québec (*November 3, 1783 to June 3, 1784*)

❧ When the MacDonalds are reunited with Angus, they also meet his friend Duncan (pp. 67–73). Mary thinks there is a mystery about Duncan. Predict what you think his story might be.

❧ Mary describes the food the family has available to them at the refugee camp at Machiche (p. 77). Compare their diet to the requirements of Canada's Food Guide. What are they missing? What health problems might they have as a result of their diet?

✍ What difficulties do the refugees face in running a school at Machiche (p. 82)? Why would the MacDonalds and Rosses be unusual in allowing their daughters to attend school?

✍ Why is it significant that Mrs. MacDonald donates baby Margaret's blanket to the Livingstones for a new quilt (p. 89)?

✍ Mary's grandmother gives her a fine embroidered handkerchief for her birthday (p. 94). Have you received any special keepsakes from your relatives?

✍ Mary mentions the different Christmas traditions of the English, the Irish and the German Loyalists. She also mentions that the Scots celebrate Hogmanay instead (pp. 95–100). Do some research to find out about the history of these traditions.

✍ Mary and her mother participate in a quilting bee (pp. 118–122). Why is the bee so important to the women of the camp?

✍ What is the significance of the fact that Grannie's lilac bush blooms (p. 128)?

Johnstown *(June 7, 1784 to November 5, 1784)*

✍ Mrs. MacDonald says that they have earned everything that Britain can give them (p. 137). Do you agree? What do you think Britain owed families like the MacDonalds?

✍ Mary describes the process by which the Loyalists were given land (pp. 136–143). Do you think this was a fair way to distribute land?

✍ Mrs. MacDonald says that the location of their cabin is a good spot (p. 147). How has her attitude changed over the course of the diary? Why do you think she has changed?

✍ Use Mary's description of the building of the cabin to write step-by-step instructions with illustrations (pp. 152–160).

✍ Some Mississauga Indians come and trade with the MacDonalds (pp. 163–164). Make a chart listing what the Loyalists learned from the Indians and what the Indians received from the Loyalists throughout the course of Mary's diary.

Canadian log house

ᘛ Make a chart showing all the members of the MacDonald family and the chores they do in order to set up a home on their land.

ᘛ Mary finally solves the mystery of Duncan (pp. 181–184). Write a letter that Duncan might write to his family in Albany, explaining why he supported the British Crown and describing his new life.

Making wood ashes for potash

—•— Activities —•—

• Note all the locations Mary mentions on her journey. On the reproducible map provided (p. 15) trace the route the MacDonald family took from Albany to Johnstown. Calculate the actual distance the family travelled over the course of a year.

• Find out about typical weather patterns in Albany. Will the MacDonalds be prepared for the weather in Québec based on their experience in Albany?

• Make a list of all the folk remedies that Grannie makes or suggests (eg. goose grease to heal blisters). See particularly the list on pages 138 to 140. Research to find out if and why they work.

• Record all the dangers that the MacDonald family and other Loyalists faced on their journey and in making a new life at Johnstown (eg. illness, injury, drowning in rivers, fire). Create a Settler Safety Guide to help the Loyalists cope with or avoid these dangers.

- Find out more about Joseph Brant. Based on the information you discover, write a job advertisement for "Chief of the Six Nations."
  Find out more about Molly Brant, too.

- Learn the song "The Golden Vanity," and other traditional sea shanties.

- Find out more about the Loyalists who came to Québec and to Nova Scotia. Create a pie chart showing the ethnic backgrounds of these Loyalists.

- List all the ways that the Loyalists depend on each other and on the military. Find out about Governor Haldimand.

- Have a "Loyalist" bee to work together on a community project (like the quilting and logging bees in the diary). Accompany your celebration with the food Mary mentions in the book, such as johnnycake and maple syrup.

- Draw pictures of the most significant episodes in the diary on quilt squares. Put the quilt together and display it in the classroom.

- Make a model or diorama of the MacDonalds' farm as it would have looked in October, 1784.

- Write a letter that Mary might have written to her former friend Lizzie in Albany, telling her about her new life in Québec.

- Complete the MacDonald family tree with the information in the Epilogue.

Domestic spinning
and weaving

Name _____

Mary's Loyalist Journey

Trace the route that the MacDonald family took from Albany to Johnstown.

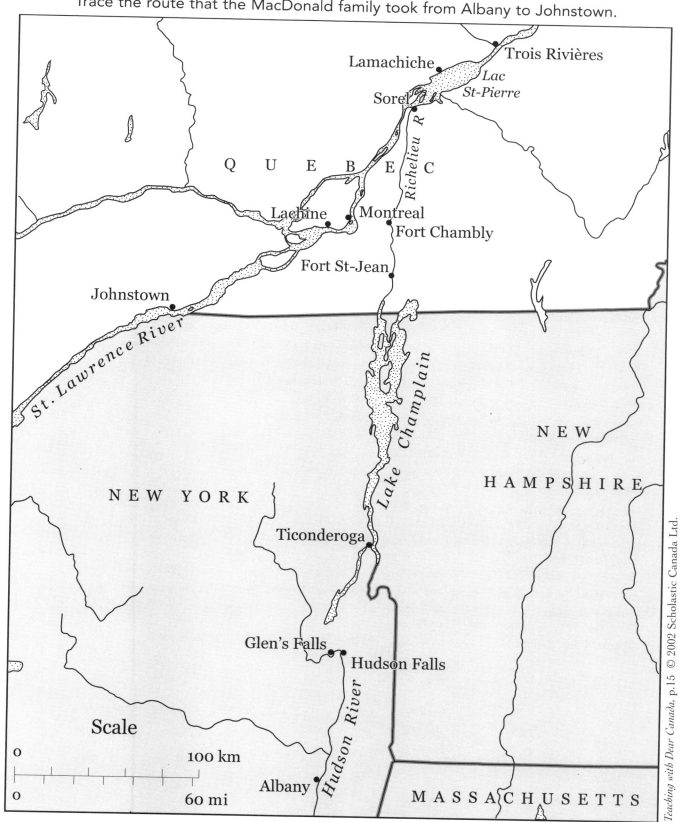

Trois Rivières

Lamachiche

Lac St-Pierre

Sorel

Richelieu R.

Q U E B E C

Lachine

Montreal

Fort Chambly

Fort St-Jean

Johnstown

St. Lawrence River

Lake Champlain

N E W   H A M P S H I R E

N E W   Y O R K

Ticonderoga

Glen's Falls

Hudson Falls

Scale

Hudson River

| 0 | | | | 100 km |

| 0 | | | | 60 mi |

Albany

M A S S A C H U S E T T S

With Nothing But Our Courage
The Loyalist Diary of Mary MacDonald

— Bibliography —

Non-fiction
Bolton, Jonathan. (1992). *Joseph Brant: Mohawk Chief.* New York: Chelsea House.

Greenwood, Barbara. (1994). *A Pioneer Story.* Toronto: Kids Can Press.

Livesey, Robert. (1999). *The Loyal Refugees.* Toronto: Stoddart Kids.

Lunn, Janet and Moore, Christopher. (1992). *The Story of Canada.* Toronto: Lester.

Neering, Rosemary and Garrod, Stan. (1975). *Life of the Loyalists.* Toronto: Fitzhenry & Whiteside.

Fiction
Collier, James. (1974). *My Brother Sam Is Dead.* New York: Scholastic.

Crook, Connie Brummel. (2001). *The Hungry Year.* Toronto: Stoddart Kids.

Downie, Mary Alice and Downie, John. (1971). *Honor Bound.* Toronto: Oxford.

Fryer, Mary Beacock. (1988). *Beginning Again: Adventures of a Loyalist Family.* Toronto: Dundurn Press.

Fryer, Mary Beacock. (2000). *Escape: Adventures of a Loyalist Family.* Toronto: Boardwalk Books.

Goodman, Joan E. (1998). *Hope's Crossing.* New York: Puffin Books.

Lunn, Janet. (1999). *Charlotte.* Toronto: Tundra Books.

Lunn, Janet. (1997). *The Hollow Tree.* Toronto: Alfred A. Knopf.

O'Dell, Scott. (1980). *Sarah Bishop.* Boston: Houghton Mifflin.

Smyth, Donna. (1991). *Loyalist Runaway.* Halifax: Formac.

Turner, Ann. (1992). *Katie's Trunk.* New York: Simon & Schuster.

Background Information for Teachers
Buchberg, Wendy. (1996). *Quilting Activities Across the Curriculum.* New York: Scholastic.

Kelsay, Isabel Thompson. (1984). *Joseph Brant, 1743–1807, Man of Two Worlds.* Syracuse, N.Y.: Syracuse University Press.

Moore, Christopher. (1994). *The Loyalists: Revolution, Exile and Settlement.* Toronto: McClelland & Stewart.

Paul, Ann Whitford. (1991). *Eight Hands Round: A Patchwork Alphabet.* New York: Harper Collins.

Potter-McKinnon, Janice. (1993). *While the Women Only Wept: Loyalist Refugee Women in Eastern Ontario.* Montreal: McGill-Queen's University Press.

Thomas, Earle. (1996). *The Three Faces of Molly Brant: A Biography.* Kingston: Quarry Press.

Footsteps in the Snow

The Red River Diary of Isobel Scott

Rupert's Land, 1815

Summary: Twelve-year-old Isobel Scott travels from the Highlands of Scotland to Rupert's Land in July, 1815. Though her mother has died, Isobel, her father and her brothers are determined to make a success of their new life at Lord Selkirk's colony at Red River. When they arrive at the Hudson's Bay Company fort of York Factory, however, they discover that they have landed in the middle of a battle between two fur trading companies. Though the settlement at The Forks has already been destroyed once by the North West Company, the Scotts travel there in York boats in order to build the colony again. Upon arriving at The Forks, the Scotts learn that they must continue their journey with Red River carts to winter at Fort Daer at Pembina. During the winter the new colonists depend almost entirely on the generosity of the aboriginal people, who share their food and their skills to see that the newcomers survive. Isobel is troubled by the friendship she feels for people she thinks are "savages," and her resentment toward them only increases when her father decides to marry White Loon, a Cree woman. When Isobel's family returns to The Forks in the spring, they try to settle into their new home. The increasing tension between the Hudson's Bay Company and the North West Company, however, makes that difficult. When the massacre at Seven Oaks occurs in June, 1816, it becomes clear how vulnerable the colonists are. After another difficult winter, in June, 1817, the Scotts return permanently to The Forks. Isobel realizes how much she has come to identify with her new land and with its aboriginal people.

What's Going On in the World in 1815?

— The Treaty of Ghent (1814) finally ended the War of 1812 between Britain and the United States. The Battle of New Orleans is fought in 1815, before news of the peace treaty arrives in North America. Communities along the Canada–U.S. border start to return to normal life.

— Napoleon escapes Elba and returns to France, only to be defeated at Waterloo.

— Brazil declares itself an independent empire.

— Romantics Byron, Wordsworth and Scott publish poems and novels.

— Humphrey Davy invents the miner's safety lamp.

— British road surveyor John Macadam constructs roads of crushed stones.

—— Prior Knowledge ——

Ask students to consider the difference between immigrants, refugees and colonists. Discuss why the Highland Scots were seen as the sort of people who would be well-suited to building a British colony abroad. Give students an opportunity to research the climate and conditions of the Highlands and to learn about the Clearances of the early 19th century. Explain that the colonists who came to the Red River area probably did not speak English and almost certainly would not have read or written English. Rather, they were Gaelic speakers. Discuss the difficulties this historical fact might have created for the author of the diary, Carol Matas. How did she overcome these difficulties? Is her explanation for Isobel's ability to read and write English plausible? Introduce students to Thomas Douglas, Lord Selkirk, and discuss his previous attempts to resettle Highlanders in Prince Edward Island and Upper Canada. Explain why the territory Isobel is settling in was called "Rupert's Land." Find the territory on a contemporary map of Canada. Ask students to predict what difficulties colonists might have faced in their journey from Britain to York Factory and in their attempts to establish a community at The Forks. Discuss the possible significance of the title of Isobel Scott's diary, *Footsteps in the Snow*.

—— Discussion Questions ——

The Voyage *(July 15, 1815 to August 27, 1815)*

On the journey, Isobel's father tells her the story of how he met her mother (p. 7). Isobel has heard the story many times before. Why does she encourage him to repeat it again? Why is it an important story for the family? Do you have family stories that seem to be told time and time again? Why are they significant for your family?

☙ Isobel is asked to assist the teacher because her English skills are good (p. 9). Most of the people on the ship would have spoken Gaelic and probably would not have read or written either language. Why do you think Isobel's English is good?

☙ Isobel begins to feel very "closed in" (p. 12) on the ship. Find out how cramped a ship like the *Prince of Wales* would have been.

☙ Kate McGilvery thinks that Isobel is too haughty (p. 16). What evidence have you read that might suggest that Isobel is too proud?

Arrival at York Factory
(August 28, 1815 to September 3, 1815)

☙ Use Isobel's description of the fort (pp. 20–21) to sketch what you think it looks like. Compare your sketch with a picture of the fort.

York Factory

☙ Find out what all the furs Isobel mentions were used for (p. 26).

On the Hayes River
(September 6, 1815 to October 15, 1815)

☙ Why is Isobel so scared of Running Fox (pp. 29–30)?

☙ Make a list of everything Isobel mentions eating on the journey. Who supplies the food?

On to Pembina *(November 3, 1815 to November 15, 1815)*

☙ Jasper McKay plays his bagpipes at important moments on the trip (p. 39). Why does he do this?

☙ What new food does Isobel try at The Forks (pp. 42–43)?

☙ Why does Isobel say that Running Fox has a "foxy" smile (p. 43)?

☙ How would you describe Isobel's attitude toward the aboriginal girl she trades with (pp. 46–47)? Describe that episode from the point of view of the aboriginal girl.

☙ Kate rescues Robbie when she has a feeling that something is wrong (pp. 51–54). Why is this called having a "sixth sense?" Do you think it is possible to have such a gift?

Winter at Pembina *(November 16, 1815 to May 4, 1816)*

❧ Kate seems to bother Isobel constantly, but also seems to want to be her friend (p. 58). Create a short biography for Kate that accounts for her strange behaviour.

❧ Isobel seems determined to take her mother's place in the family. List all the things she does that her mother would have done for the family (pp. 61–67).

❧ Why would Kate be frightened of static electricity (pp. 67–68)?

❧ Describe Isobel's attitude toward White Loon (pp. 69–70). Why do you think she feels this way?

❧ Why do you think Isobel and the other settlers are so upset about the extent to which they depend on their Cree neighbours (pp. 70–74)? How does White Loon try to make Isobel feel better?

❧ Why don't the Scotts celebrate Christmas? Find out about Handsel Monday and Hogmanay (pp. 70–72).

❧ Why do you think Isobel has such mixed feelings about enjoying the game she played with White Loon and the other women (p. 78)? How does she think her mother would want her to behave? Why?

❧ What evidence can you find that Isobel is beginning to rethink her attitude toward aboriginal people?

❧ Based on the information Isobel provides, describe the roles of men and women in the Cree community. Check some non-fiction sources to challenge or confirm this account.

❧ Why is Isobel so upset that her father is going to marry White Loon (p. 99)?

Red River colonists greeted by Saulteaux Indians

Settling at The Forks *(May 15, 1816 to June 23, 1816)*

❧ Write a newspaper account of the massacre at Seven Oaks (pp. 114–119). How does this differ from Isobel's version?

Leaving The Forks *(June 24, 1816 to March 3, 1816)*

❧ Isobel learns more about Kate when she meets her brother William (pp. 123–129). Why does this new information about Kate's family change Isobel's opinion of Kate?

✐ Why are the documents that White Loon was hiding so important to the North West Company (pp. 125–130)? Why can Duncan Cameron be charged with treason?

✐ When Isobel meets the Swampy Cree women near Jack River, she realizes she must not be quick to jump to judgments about them (pp. 137–138). Why has her attitude toward aboriginal people changed so much in the course of a year?

✐ Isobel comments on the naming traditions of the Cree (p. 138) and wonders what name she might make up for herself. What name do you think she should have? What name would you give yourself?

✐ It is clear that Isobel has learned a lot about herself and others in the year she has spent in the Red River area. Her younger brother Robbie has also changed a lot since his last birthday (p. 144). Describe how and why you think he has changed.

✐ In what way is Isobel's theatrical like the aboriginal story-telling tradition (p. 145)?

✐ Isobel notes that White Loon has saved both her and Robbie in the past few months (p. 151). In what other ways has she contributed to the life of the Scotts?

Back at The Forks
(June 19, 1816 to July 18, 1816)

✐ In her final diary entry, Isobel celebrates the two women who have taught her most about life: her mother and White Loon (p. 153). In a T-chart, list

Old Fort Douglas, Red River, 1816

the qualities and skills you think Isobel has learned from her mother and from White Loon.

✐ Why do you think Isobel's diary is called *Footsteps in the Snow*? In what way has she left her mark on her new country?

—◦— Activities —◦—

• Learn more about the conflict between the Nor'westers and the colonists at Red River. On the reproducible provided (p. 23), summarize the positions of the Hudson's Bay Company, the North West Company and the Red River colonists who were caught in the middle of the dispute. Use that information to: 1) write a speech a Nor'wester might have given trying to dissuade Highlanders from coming to Red

River; 2) write an advertisement the HBC might have created trying to encourage colonists to come; or 3) write a business letter from the Red River colonists to either the HBC or the NWC asking them to settle their conflict.

- Have half the class find out more about Hudson's Bay Company founders Radisson and Groseilliers, or about HBC employees such as Henry Kelsey, Anthony Henday and Peter Fidler. The other half can research the North West Company and men such as Alexander Henry, Alexander Mackenzie, David Thompson and Peter Pond. After completing their research, ask the class which company ultimately won the "fur trade war" in Rupert's Land. Challenge them to defend their answer with the information they found in their research.

- Examine the coat of arms of the province of Manitoba. Based on what you have learned about Manitoba's history, explain the significance of the symbols.

- Find out more about Cuthbert Grant, who led the Métis at Seven Oaks and later became a protector of the colony at Red River. Use the information you found to discuss whether or not a statue of Grant should be built at the site of the Red River colony.

- Use a clean pizza box to display maps of the territory that Isobel covered in her diary (York Factory on Hudson Bay, down the Hayes River to Lake Winnipeg, and down the Red River to the U.S. border). On the base of the box, make a relief map out of salt dough, showing all the landforms such as deltas, river valleys and plateaus. On drawing paper on the cover, draw a political map that shows the forts and settlements. Make generalizations about the impact of the physical landscape on patterns of settlement and trade.

- Make a diorama showing a buffalo hunt. Draw a diagram of a buffalo, labelling each part and its use.

- Using the reproducible provided (p. 24), list things that the Scotts received or learned from the aboriginal people they met, and things that the aboriginal people received or learned from them.

- Have a celebration of music and dance from the Red River colony. Listen to and dance some reels and jigs. Learn the Red River jig (a combination of a Scottish reel and Cree dance). Accompany your celebration with food described in the diary.

- As a class, create skits and songs that tell the story of the Scott family's first year at the Red River colony (like Isobel's theatrical).

- Create a timeline showing the events of the Scotts' life described in the Epilogue.

Name _____

— Points of View —

Hudson's Bay Company

"We think Red River is an important colony because . . . "

_____
_____
_____
_____
_____
_____
_____
_____
_____
_____
_____
_____
_____
_____

Red River colonists

"We just want to . . . "

_____
_____
_____
_____
_____
_____
_____
_____
_____
_____
_____
_____
_____

North West Company

"The Red River colony is a threat to us because . . . "

_____
_____
_____
_____
_____
_____
_____
_____
_____
_____
_____
_____
_____

Name _____

What Have They Learned From Each Other?

Aboriginal People

Isobel and the Scott family

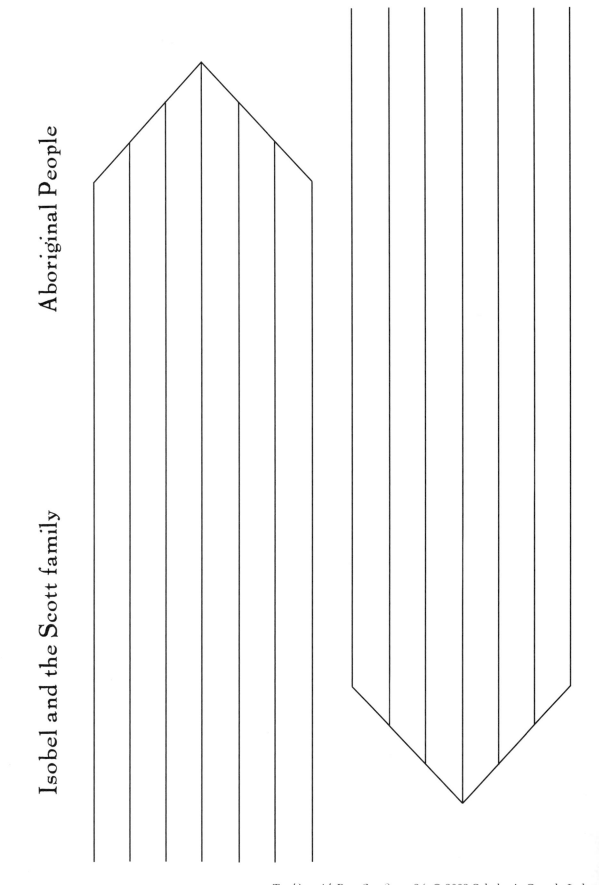

Footsteps in the Snow
The Red River Diary of Isobel Scott

—•— Bibliography —•—

Non-fiction

Duquemin, Colin K. (1992). *The Fur Trade in Rupert's Land: Opening Up the Canadian Northwest.* St. Catharines: Vanwell Publishing.

Grant, Agnes. (1994). *James McKay: A Métis Builder of Canada.* Winnipeg: Pemmican Publications.

Hancock, Pat. (1999). *The Penguin Book of Canadian Biography for Young Readers: Early Canada.* Toronto: Viking.
— see entry for Thomas Douglas, Lord Selkirk.

Livesey, Robert and Smith, A.G. (1989). *The Fur Traders.* Toronto: Stoddart.

Lunn, Janet and Moore, Christopher. (1992). *The Story of Canada.* Toronto: Lester.

Mercredi, Morningstar. (1997). *Fort Chipewyan Homecoming.* Minneapolis: Lerner.
— a look at a contemporary Cree community

Moore, Christopher. (2000). *Adventurers: Hudson's Bay Company — the Epic Story.* Toronto: Quantum Book Group.

Neering, Rosemary. (1974). *Fur Trade.* Toronto: Fitzhenry and Whiteside.

Wilson, Keith. (1983). *The Red River Settlement.* Toronto: Grolier.

Fiction

Bellingham, Brenda. (1985). *Storm Child.* Toronto: Lorimer.
— in the 1830s, Isobel comes to terms with her mixed heritage and the impact of the fur trade on western Canada.

Demers, Barbara. (1999). *Willa's New World.* Regina: Coteau Books.
— a fifteen-year-old girl travels to York Factory in 1795.

Background Information for Teachers

Brown, Jennifer. (1980). *Strangers in Blood: Fur Trade Company Families in Indian Country.* Vancouver: University of British Columbia Press.

Bumsted, J.M. (1999). *Fur Trade Wars: The Founding of Western Canada.* Winnipeg: Great Plains Publishing.

Friesen, Gerald. (1984). *The Canadian Prairies: A History.* Toronto: University of Toronto Press.

Newman, Peter C. (1987). *Caesars of the Wilderness.* Markham: Viking.

Prebble, John. (1963). *The Highland Clearances.* London: Secker & Warburg.
— still the best explanation of the clearances that forced colonists like the Scotts to leave the Highlands and come to Red River.

Orphan at My Door

The Home Child Diary of Victoria Cope

Guelph, Ontario, 1897

Summary: Victoria Cope receives a diary for her eleventh birthday and begins to record the events of her daily life in late 19th century Guelph. Her father is a physician and she has two older brothers. When their maid leaves, Victoria's parents agree to take in a Home Child as domestic help. More hands around the home are especially helpful when Victoria's great-aunt and cousin join the household as well. But while some members of the household and the community look down on Home Children and treat them poorly, Victoria soon gets to know Marianna well. She learns about her difficult life in Britain, the tragedies that her family faced, and the trauma she endured when she was separated from her brother and sister. When Victoria discovers that Marianna's brother Jasper has escaped from a farmer who has been abusing him, the girls try to rescue him. Victoria's friendship with Marianna helps her realize how lucky she has been and how sheltered she has been from the realities of life.

What's Going On in the World in 1897?

— The population of the Yukon booms as men search for fortunes in gold in the Klondike.

— The first American comic strip, "The Katzenjammer Kids," is created.

— Puccini and Verdi are composing operas.

— J.J. Thomson discovers the electron.

— India suffers a severe famine.

— The first photographs using artificial light are taken.

— Prior Knowledge —

Introduce students to life in late 19th century Canada by showing photographs of cities and of rural areas, of children and of adults, and inviting them to make observations. Help them understand that in an era before modern medicine and social welfare programs, people of all backgrounds were vulnerable to disease, to injury and to poverty. In an era before the invention of many labour-saving devices, many people did physically demanding work and worked very long hours. Even housework demanded enormous physical strength and an extraordinary amount of time. Help students understand that just like today, people's lives were largely determined by their financial status. That said, the poor of the late 19th century did not have access to any government-funded support programs. They were dependent on charity and were often reminded that their poverty was their own fault. Review the notion of social "class" and the stereotypes of these notions. Talk about the stigma of poverty today and the extent to which many people still believe that poor people could improve their lives "if they just worked harder." Introduce students to charitable organizations of the 19th century, particularly those that worked with children and the poor, like Dr. Barnardo's organization. Draw their attention to contemporary organizations and the work they do.

— Discussion Questions —

☞ This diary is called the "Home Child" diary of Victoria Cope, but she is not the Home Child. Why isn't this the home child's diary?

☞ Victoria says that boys' chores are definite, but girls' chores never finish (p. 4). Is this still true?

☞ Who are the people in Victoria's family (pp. 4–8)? What "class" do you think her family belongs to? Why?

☞ Why would there have been so many babies in the graveyard (p. 6)?

☞ Victoria obviously likes stories and likes to write. What does she mean when she says that "stories are not the same as lies?" (p. 9) Do you agree with her?

☞ Victoria's mother tells her that "writers have to make the truth interesting" (p. 11). What does she mean by this? Note how Jean Little does this throughout the diary.

☞ Predict what might be the matter with Victoria's mother (p. 11).

ᔏ Why do you think the maid Peggy is upset when she gets the wedding ring in the cake (p. 10)? Why does she quit so quickly to get married (p. 15)?

ᔏ What is Victoria's view of Home Children (p. 12)? What are her family members' views (pp. 18–19)? Do some research to find out why these orphans were called Home Children.

ᔏ Victoria says that her brothers get away with things that she would be scolded for (p. 23). Why might that be? Is this still true?

ᔏ Why are Great-Aunt Lib's and cousin Anna's plans to stay with the Cope family announced in the newspaper (p. 27)?

ᔏ Reread pages 27 to 41, the story of Mary Anna's arrival at the train station to her first Sunday service. Imagine that you are Mary Anna and list all the things that were done or said that you would find humiliating. Why did the Copes treat Mary Anna this way?

ᔏ Compare and contrast your Sunday routine with the Cope family's (pp. 32–41).

ᔏ If Aunt Lib was in charge of the household, what do you think Mary Anna's life would be like (pp. 44–49)? Why?

ᔏ Mary Anna was sent to Canada with a trunk of clothes (pp. 46–47). What might the Barnardo people have included in the trunk to make the children feel more at home in Canada?

Immigrant children from Dr. Barnardo's Homes at landing stage, Saint John, N.B.

- Why would the teacher put Mary Anna in the back row with the "idiots and foreigners and the foundling boy" (p. 50)? What does Victoria mean when she uses those words?

- Why does Victoria's opinion of cousin Anna change when she knows about her background (pp. 53–59)?

- Why would the Barnardo people separate Mary Anna from her brother and sister? Do you think this was fair?

Hazel Brae, Peterborough, Ontario

- Why didn't Marianna tell the Copes what her real name was as soon as she met them (p. 71)? How would you feel if people called you by the wrong name all the time?

- As Victoria gets to know Marianna she starts to feel embarrassed and angry about her own life and her privileges (p. 76). Why would she feel this way?

- Why would a mustard plaster make someone with a cold feel better (p. 79)?

- Marianna tells Victoria the story of her parents and then says, "when no one knows, you feel as though part of you doesn't exist" (p. 85). Do you think that's true?

- Marianna briefly describes the workhouse she was in (p. 85). Do some research to find out more about workhouses in Victorian England.

- Why didn't her parents tell Victoria that her mother is pregnant (p. 90)? Why do you think adults at this time told children so little about "the facts of life" (pp. 99–100)?

- In what ways are Aunt Lib and Cousin Anna like Marianna? They also depend on the kindness of the Copes. Why aren't they more grateful?

- Why would the teacher disapprove of Victoria's choice of poem for her recitation (p. 103)? Why would he have approved of Marianna's poem?

- It is very difficult for Victoria and Marianna to find out if Pansy Jordan's Home Child is Jasper (pp. 105–113). Why don't they just write her a letter and ask?

- Victoria has come to recognize that Home Children are essentially just like her (p. 114). Why do you think this is so difficult for her brother David to understand?

∂ Victoria wishes that Jasper could find out what a real Canadian home is like (p. 118). What do you think a real home should be like for children like Jasper?

∂ Carl Stone is obviously abusing Jasper. Why wouldn't Jasper run away? Why wouldn't he ask someone for help? Write a letter in which Jasper describes his life with Mr. Stone and asks for help.

∂ Tom is furious with Mr. Stone when he finds out about Jasper (p. 139). Marianna reminds him that "women and children have no say when it comes to things like this." Is she right? Find out what rights women and children had in Canada in 1897.

∂ Why is Victoria scared when her mother is ordered to stay in bed until she gives birth (p. 151)?

∂ Marianna is obviously very worried about her brother and yet she continues to take care of the Cope household. How do you think she manages to do that? What evidence can you find that the family's attitudes towards Marianna have changed since they first met her?

∂ Why do you think Victoria would want to name her new sister after Marianna's sister?

∂ Marianna turns thirteen and considers herself a woman (p. 187). Victoria sees no evidence of this. In what ways is Marianna grown up? In what ways is she still a girl?

∂ Why does Mrs. Cope feel she owes it to Marianna's mother to see that Marianna goes to school (p. 189)?

∂ Victoria closes her diary with a poem about thankfulness. After reading about the lives of children in the 1890s, what are you thankful for? Write your own poem about thankfulness.

— Activities —

- In 1897 Queen Victoria celebrated her Diamond Jubilee. Indicate on a map of the world the extent of the British Empire of which Canada was a part.

- Victoria records many 19th century aphorisms in her diary:
  - "A man can work from sun to sun, but woman's work is never done."
  - "Give him enough rope and he'll hang himself."
  - "Be good, sweet maid, and let who can be clever.
    Do noble things, not dream them, all day long . . . "
  - "Cleanliness is next to godliness."
  - "No rest for the wicked."
  - "The shoemaker's child goes barefoot."
  - "There's a fool born every minute."
  - "There's no fool like an old fool."
  - "The Devil finds work for idle hands."

  Make a book of these sayings with illustrations and explanations.

- Make a mobile that illustrates all the members of the Cope household and their roles in the family.

- Write a story about the life of Emily Rose (Marianna's sister) after she was separated from her siblings.

- Compare and contrast the lives of Victoria and Marianna (or Tom and Jasper) on the reproducible chart provided (p. 33). On a separate piece of paper, write three generalizations about the lives of privileged children and of working children based on the chart. Use the information you recorded to compare and contrast the lives and responsibilities of girls and boys of that era, or to compare and contrast their lives to yours.

- Have a school concert and recite poems of Robert Louis Stevenson or others that Victoria mentions. Afterwards, have wheelbarrow and potato sack races. Serve specialties of the time such as burnt leather cake.

- Read some of the novels that Victoria mentions, such as *Little Women*, *Little Men*, *The Water Babies* and *Eight Cousins*. How do these novels compare to those written today? In what way does Victoria's diary sound like the 19th century novels?

- Make a collage that illustrates Marianna's contributions to the Cope family household. Write a story that explains what life in the Cope family would have been like in the summer of 1897 if Marianna had never arrived.

- Write diary entries that David might have written that illustrate how his attitudes toward Marianna and Jasper changed from May to September 1897.

- Do some research about the rights of children today, particularly about the United Nations Convention on the Rights of the Child. Would Canada be able to bring child immigrants to the country today? Why or why not? How would Marianna's and Jasper's lives have been different if the Convention had been in effect in 1897?

- What happens to children like Marianna and Jasper today? Find out about social welfare agencies and charitable organizations that help children in your community. Take on a class project to support a hot lunch program, collect warm coats for children, or do another project to make a difference in the lives of children.

- Do some research about child labour around the world and the activists who are trying to stop the practice. In what parts of the world do children work? What kind of work do they do? How does their labour benefit their families? How would their lives change if they did not work?

Girls leaving Hazel Brae

Name _____

— The Lives of Children in 1897 —

Victoria	Marianna

Housing

Daily routine

Chores

Leisure activities

Schooling

Toys

Teaching with Dear Canada, p. 33 © 2002 Scholastic Canada Ltd.

Orphan
at My Door
The Home Child Diary of Victoria Cope

— Bibliography —

Non-fiction

Castle, Caroline. (2000). *For Every Child: The UN Convention on the Rights of the Child in Words and Pictures.* London: Hutchinson.

Freedman, Russell. (1980). *Immigrant Kids.* New York: Dutton.

Granfield, Linda. (2000). *Pier 21: Gateway of Hope.* Toronto: Tundra Books.

Lunn, Janet and Moore, Christopher. (1992). *The Story of Canada.* Toronto: Lester.

Parker, David L. et al. (1998). *Stolen Dreams: Portraits of Working Children.* Minneapolis: Lerner Publications.

Springer, Jane. (1997). *Listen to Us: The World's Working Children.* Toronto: Douglas & McIntyre.

Wicks, Ben. (1989). *No Time to Wave Goodbye.* Toronto: Stoddart.

Fiction

Bunting, Eve. (1996). *Train to Somewhere.* New York: Clarion Books.

Doherty, Berlie. (1993). *Street Child.* New York: HarperCollins.

Hamilton, Mary. (1998). *The Tin-Lined Trunk.* Toronto: Kids Can Press.

Harrison, Troon. (2000). *A Bushel of Light.* Toronto: Stoddart Kids.

Haworth-Attard, Barbara. (1996). *Home Child.* Montreal: Roussan.

Holeman, Linda. (1997). *Promise Song.* Toronto: Tundra Books.

Horne, Constance. (1998). *The Accidental Orphan.* Vancouver: Beach Holme.

Background Information for Teachers

Bagnall, Kenneth. (2001). *The Little Immigrants: The Orphans Who Came to Canada.* Toronto: Dundurn Press.

Corbett, Gail H. (1997). *Barnardo Children in Canada.* Peterborough: Woodland Publishers.

Harrison, Phyllis, ed. (1979). *The Home Children: Their Personal Stories.* Winnipeg: Watson & Dwyer.

Kielberger, Craig with Major, Kevin. (1998). *Free the Children: A Young Man Fights Against Child Labor and Proves that Children Can Change the World.* Toronto: McClelland and Stewart.

Newman, Peter C. (1992). *Canada — 1892: Portrait of a Promised Land.* Toronto: Madison Press.

Parr, Joy. (1994). *Labouring Children: British Immigrant Apprentices to Canada, 1869-1924.* Toronto: University of Toronto Press.

Wagner, Gillian. (1979). *Barnardo.* Eyre & Spottiswoode.

A Prairie as Wide as the Sea

The Immigrant Diary of Ivy Weatherall

Milorie, Saskatchewan, 1926

Summary: Eleven-year-old Ivy Weatherall leaves her home in London, England, with her family to settle on the Canadian prairies. After travelling on the *Ausonia* from London to Québec City, Ivy and her family travel by train to Milorie, Saskatchewan, near Maple Creek. Over the course of a year, Ivy's family learns that life in western Canada is not exactly as it was advertised in England. Farm life is difficult and certainly not as lucrative as it was made out to be. Every member of the family must contribute to the family income, taking any job, no matter how menial, in order to make a living. And there are adjustments to make in terms of culture and language, too. Who knew that people who speak the same language could mean such different things! Ivy comes to appreciate life in her prairie community, and by the end of her first year in Saskatchewan, realizes how Canadian she has become.

What's Going On in the World in 1926?

~ Magician Harry Houdini is killed when a McGill University student punches him and ruptures his spleen.

~ Canada has 75,200 kilometres of paved road.

~ Townspeople and railway workers save the Banff Springs Hotel from fire.

~ Prohibition enforcement officials in New York find 138 cases of champagne under a shipment of P.E.I. potatoes.

~ *Winnie the Pooh* is published.

~ "Jelly Roll" Morton's and Duke Ellington's first jazz recordings appear.

~ The German airline Lufthansa is created.

Prior Knowledge

Ask students to define the term "immigrant." Encourage them to share stories of their own families' journeys to Canada or talk about groups of immigrants they may have learned about before. Discuss why people throughout Canada's history have chosen to leave their homes and settle here. Help students understand that people came to Canada in the 1920s for many of the same reasons they come today: to find better opportunities for themselves and their children. Explain that Canadian governments throughout history have made immigration policy to encourage the "right sort" of people to come to Canada. If appropriate, discuss with the students the kind of people the government was looking for in terms of race, language and work background, and the impact this might have had on the development of the country. Provide the students with some background information about plans such as The Empire Settlement Act of 1922 and Canadian Pacific Railway settlement plans, in order to illustrate how the government and other organizations attracted people to western Canada. Ask students to predict what kinds of problems might arise through schemes like these.

Discussion Questions

Preparing to Leave *(May 1, 1926 to May 2, 1926)*

In her first diary entry, Ivy makes a promise to herself that she will never forget what it's like to be a child (p. 4). Do you think most adults forget what it's like to be a child? What do you think that means? Explain your answer.

Why do you think medical officers examined the people getting on the ship (p. 5)? What do you think the consequences would be if they found someone who was ill?

The Voyage *(May 2, 1926, Later to May 19, 1926)*

Ivy's family is "working class." What do you think this means? Why is she angry when her father implies that they are poor (p. 6)? How would you define "poor"?

Why is the ship divided into classes? What are the differences between the classes?

How do the passengers amuse themselves on board?

Mr. Weatherall reads a Canada West booklet that "tells us everything we need to know" about settling in Canada (p. 13). Do you think it really tells everything? Why or why not? Make some predictions about the hardships and rewards the family will find in Saskatchewan. The booklet also outlines who is not allowed in Canada (p. 14). Discuss what kinds of people the government probably would not want to allow to enter into Canada. How would they identify such people?

In Winnipeg Ivy learns something about prejudice. She sees a Chinese person for the first time and realizes that the Chinese are not as scary as the magazines portray them. What stereotypes of people have you seen in books, magazines, television or movies? Why are those images so powerful? Then she sees a sign on a livery stable that says, "Help Wanted. Englishmen Need Not Apply" (p. 18). Why do you think some Canadians might have been prejudiced against the English in the 1920s?

Arrival *(Still May 19, 1926 to May 23, 1926)*

Milorie is a small town in rural Saskatchewan. Using Ivy's description on page 20, sketch a map of the town, or, using her description on p. 21, sketch Uncle Alf's homestead. Discuss how life in this community is going to differ from the life that Ivy was used to in London.

The Weatheralls quickly discover the truth about Uncle Alf. Why do you think he has had so little success in Canada? Why is everyone angry with him? Does the truth about Uncle Alf explain some of the prejudice against the English that the Weatheralls encountered in Winnipeg?

Making Adjustments

(May 25, 1926 to June 27, 1926)

William works at the general store to support the family and to pay off his uncle's debts (pp. 33–34). Why do you think he (at fourteen years of age) must get a job? Is that fair? Compare and contrast the work he does with the work of grocery store clerks today. Would we allow fourteen-year-olds to do that job?

Joe Beauchamp store — Qu'Appelle, Saskatchewan, 1920s

Ivy makes a mistake that could cost her family a lot of money when she orders cotton cloth at the general store, instead of thread (p. 35). What other misunderstandings does she face? Discuss how people who speak the same language can mean different things. Share examples of words or expressions that can mean one thing to one group of people and something different to another. Have you ever faced misunderstandings like these?

Life on the Prairies *(July 1, 1926 to October 24, 1926)*

On July 1 the Weatheralls celebrate Dominion Day (pp. 51–52). Now we call this Canada Day. When did the name change? Why? Her father sings "The Maple Leaf Forever." Find the lyrics for the song and discuss what they mean. Why do you think that song did not become Canada's official national anthem? Identify Ireland, Scotland, England and Wales on a map. Discuss their places in the United Kingdom.

Why do the boys in Milorie think William is stuck up? Ivy thinks it is harder for William to make friends than for her (p. 70). Why do you think that might be?

William says that despite the hardships, he wants to stay in Canada. In Canada he can become "somebody." What do you think he means by that? What kind of person do you think William will become? Predict what you think he and Ivy will do in the future (and don't peek in the Epilogue!).

When Lorayne LaMott comes to visit her uncle in Milorie, Ivy is very impressed with her, but her mother says that she is, "no better than she ought to be" (p. 80). What do you think this means? Why is Ivy so impressed with her?

While Ivy and her younger brother and sister are going to school, William is working. Ivy says that her brother "is working like a grown-up man" and that this makes her sad (p. 93). Why do you think immigrant children had to grow up so quickly?

Elizabeth's brother Gerhard hates the farm and runs away to Calgary to join a jazz band. Why do you think his father is so angry with him? Why might he be worried about Gerhard living in a city? Later he says that jazz music is "wicked music" (p. 125). What do you think he means by that? Do you think music can be wicked?

Why is Ivy so angry about leaving the farm? How do you think her life will change, living in town?

When Ivy minds the children by herself during the blizzard, her father says that she has become "very Canadian" (p. 108). What do you think he means by that? What does Ivy learn about herself during that episode?

J. Fockler barn with horses — Broadview, Saskatchewan, 1928

Being Canadian in the 1920s *(October 25, 1926 to April 16, 1927)*

✒ Compare and contrast the way Ivy celebrates Hallowe'en with the way we celebrate now. Other holidays have also changed over the years. Ivy recognizes Armistice Day and Thanksgiving Day on different dates than we do now. What is Armistice Day called now? Why did the name change? When did the date of Thanksgiving Day change? Why?

✒ In the 1920s Canada was part of the British Empire (p. 126). Find all the places Ivy mentions in her diary on a map of the world. Find a map of the world from the 1920s, and discuss the size of the Empire and what bound these countries together.

✒ When Ivy's family receives their Christmas parcel from England, they share memories of the country they have left behind. Ivy realizes that the twins will not really remember England, but that she and the others "will carry little bits of England around" for the rest of their lives (p. 141). What do you think she means by that? What "bits" will she carry around? Do you think this is true of all immigrants?

✒ School is cancelled when a boy hurts himself (p. 148). Why was an injury so dangerous then?

✒ Ivy's mother attends meetings of the Homemaker's Club (p. 157). What do you think that is? Why do you think a club like this would have been important to women on the prairies? Do some research on other women's organizations in the 1920s.

Children in front of Edgewood School — class of 1930–31

✒ At school Nyla Muir teases Ivy because of her homemade clothes and practical Christmas gifts. When Ivy visits the Mullers she envies their pictures on the walls. She thinks they have all the characteristics that the books said successful immigrants should have (p. 161). Do you think Ivy's family is poor? Why do you think they still have to work so hard?

✒ Play Elizabeth's game called point (p. 169). Think about all the games that Ivy has played and the things she has done for fun. What do you notice about them? Do they have much equipment? Are they expensive to play? Invent your own game using the most common household equipment you can find. It cannot cost money but it must be fun.

✒ How does Ivy's relationship with her mother change after she helps her deliver the baby (pp. 180–184)?

Closure *(April 18, 1927)*

✍ At the end of her first year on the prairie, Ivy has become a "big Canadian Ivy" (p. 185). She says that she is not the same girl she was a year ago. How has she changed?

✍ Why do you think Ivy's diary is called *A Prairie as Wide as the Sea*? Think about all the references to the sea and Ivy's experience with the sea. Think about her walk with Mr. Ambrose on the prairie (p. 120). Do you think this is a good metaphor to use to describe the prairie?

—— Activities ——

• Pack Ivy's trunk. What do you think she would have put into her trunk for her journey across the ocean and her new life in Canada?

• During the sea voyage, Ivy's brothers and sister laugh about the names of places in Canada, like Medicine Hat and Moose Jaw (p. 10). Research the origins of interesting Canadian place names. Later they learn how Milorie got its name (p. 33). Create names of fictional towns in Canada out of your names.

• On a map, draw the Weatherall family's journey from London, England, to Milorie, Saskatchewan. Illustrate your map with pictures of scenery the family might have seen on the journey. Draw illustrations or cut appropriate landscape pictures out of magazines.

• Create a chart that contrasts Ivy's life in London with her life in Milorie, using the reproducible provided (p. 43). When you have finished the book and the chart, use the information you have collected to write a letter from Ivy to Ethel explaining how your life has changed.

• At the end of your unit, have a special lunch featuring the "Canadian" foods Ivy ate.

  – blueberry pie   – saskatoon pie   – peanut butter
  – lutefisk   – coleslaw   – doughnuts

• Keep a glossary of all of Ivy's English expressions or words that are unfamiliar to you. Try to use them in conversation.

• When Ivy's family arrives in Milorie, they have to join Uncle Alf's family in the shanty on the homestead. On the floor, outline the dimensions of a shanty with some masking tape. Make outlines of the furniture they would have had in the shanty (wood stove, wood box, table, chairs) and place them on the floor. Now pack nine people into the remaining space. Discuss what it feels like to be crowded into that space. What challenges do you think pioneer families might have faced?

- Ivy learns how to do farm chores, including making butter (p. 31). She says that butter is made of cream and work. Try making some butter. (See p. 83 of *A Pioneer Story*). Do you agree with her?

- Make a chart showing all the jobs that Ivy, William, her mother and her father do over the course of a year to support the family.

- Come one, come all to the Chautauqua!

  – Have an opening parade in the gymnasium or outside.

  – Sing songs that are mentioned in the book, like "Life on the Ocean Wave," "What Shall We Do with a Drunken Sailor," "I'm Forever Blowing Bubbles," "Who Put the Overalls in Mrs. Murphy's Chowder?," "The Maple Leaf Forever," "On the Road to Mandalay," and "The Ash Grove."

  – Give a short lecture on a topic of interest to you (and remember to bring artifacts to enhance your presentation).

  – Perform a marionette or puppet show.

  – Recite poetry.

- Ivy's mother says that Aunt Millie should never have come to Canada, that she is not the "pioneer sort" (p. 47). What does she mean by that? What kind of person do you think is the pioneer sort? Create a job ad outlining the kind of person you think should have come to western Canada in the 1920s.

Homesteaders Peter and Edith Reimer & their children circa 1925

- Have a class Dominion Day celebration. Make a picnic. Play games like sack races and baseball. Try square dancing. Sing "The Maple Leaf Forever."

- When Mr. Ambrose moves into the Weatheralls' hotel, he asks Ivy to ask him a question every day so that he can look up the answer in his encyclopedia. Introduce a "question of the day" in your classroom.

- Ivy provides a detailed description of the Mullers' new tube radio (p. 124). There is a picture of such a radio on page 198. Draw a timeline showing changes in radio technology through the twentieth century, or choose another kind of technology.

- At the school Christmas concert, the students do an acrostic act (pp. 129–30). Write your own acrostic poems for "Ivy Weatherall" or "immigrants."

- Have a class box social (pp. 164–166).

- Find copies of the stories, books, magazines and even newspapers that Ivy mentions, or others from the 1920s. Compare and contrast them with those of our time.
  - Canadian Readers
  - *Lost in the Backwoods*, by Catharine Parr Traill
  - *Anne of Green Gables*, by Lucy Maud Montgomery
  - *At the Back of the North Wind*, by George MacDonald
  - *Sowing Seeds in Danny*, by Nellie McClung

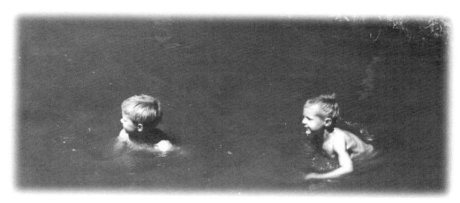

Boys swimming in a slew (or dugout)

- Compare and contrast the English games Ivy knows (quoits, rounders) with the games she learns in Canada (baseball, fox and geese).

- On a map of Canada, label all the places where the members of the family lived later in their lives.

- Create the Weatherall family tree.

Name _____

	— Life in London —	— Life in Milorie —
Food		
Clothing		
Shelter		
Recreation		
Schools		
Work		
Holidays		
Language/ Expressions		
Landscape		

A Prairie as Wide as the Sea
The Immigrant Diary of Ivy Weatherall

— Bibliography —

Non-fiction

Bercuson, David. (1980). *Opening the Canadian West*. Toronto: Grolier.

Bercuson, David. (1984). *Settling the Canadian West*. Toronto: Grolier.

Caswell, Maryanne. (2001). *Pioneer Girl*. Toronto: Tundra Books.
~ the letters in this book were written by Maryanne Caswell to her grandmother in 1887. They describe her life as a child on a prairie homestead and provide an interesting contrast with Ivy's life in the same region of the country forty years later.

Greenwood, Barbara. (1994). *A Pioneer Story*. Toronto: Kids Can Press.
~ although this book details life in Upper Canada in the 1840s, it provides good information about pioneer life and reminds students how long the "pioneer settlement" period lasted in Canada's history.

Johnston, Gordon. (1984). *It Happened in Canada*. Markham: Scholastic Canada.

Neering, Rosemary. (1985). *Settlement of the West*. Vancouver: Fitzhenry and Whiteside.

Wilson, Keith. (1985). *Album of Western Settlement*. Toronto: Grolier.

Plays

Mitchell, Ken. (1982). *Chautauqua Girl: a musical show for young people*. Toronto: Playwrights Canada.

Fiction

Beeler, Cecil Freeman. (1991). *The Girl in the Well*. Red Deer: Red Deer College Press. See also *No Room in the Well* and *Boys in the Well* by the same author.

Booth, David. (1996). *The Dust Bowl*. Toronto: Kids Can Press.

Hutchins, Hazel. (1995). *Tess*. Toronto: Annick Press.

Jam, Teddy. (1999). *The Stoneboat*. Toronto: Douglas & McIntyre.

Kurelek, William. (1975). *A Prairie Boy's Summer*. Montreal: Tundra Books.

Kurelek, William. (1973). *A Prairie Boy's Winter*. Montreal: Tundra Books.

Lottridge, Celia Barker. (1994). *Ticket to Curlew*. Vancouver: Douglas & McIntyre.

Lottridge, Celia Barker. (1997). *Wings to Fly*. Vancouver: Douglas & McIntyre.

McGugan, Jim. (1994). *Josepha*. Red Deer: Red Deer College Press.

Reynolds, Marilynn. (1993). *Belle's Journey*. Victoria: Orca Book Publishers.

Reynolds, Marilynn. (1994). *A Dog for a Friend*. Victoria: Orca Book Publishers.

Reynolds, Marilynn. (1997). *The New Land: A First Year on the Prairie*. Victoria: Orca Book Publishers.

Reynolds, Marilynn. (1999). *The Prairie Fire*. Victoria: Orca Book Publishers.

Taylor, Cora. (1987). *The Doll*. Saskatoon: Western Producer Prairie Books.

Trottier, Maxine. (1998). *Prairie Willow*. Toronto: Stoddart Kids.

Background Information for Teachers

Broadfoot, Barry. (1988). *Next-year Country: Voices of Prairie People*. Toronto: McClelland and Stewart.

Friesen, Gerald. (1987). *The Canadian Prairies: A History*. Toronto: University of Toronto Press.

Rayburn, Alan. (1999). *Dictionary of Canadian Place Names*. Toronto: Oxford University Press.

Rayburn, Alan. (2001). *Naming Canada: Stories about Canadian Place Names*. Toronto: University of Toronto Press.

Thompson, John Herd. (1998). *Forging the Prairie West*. Toronto: Oxford University Press.

— Turning Points —

As the diary progresses, the fictional author changes.
On the organizer below, describe the author's character at the beginning of the diary
and at the end. Then identify the points in the diary when she changes. Give the page
number of the turning points and brief explanations for them.

Character at the beginning _____

_____

_____

_____

_____

Turning point 1 _____

_____

_____

_____

_____

Turning point 2 _____

_____

_____

_____

_____

Character at the end _____

_____

_____

_____

_____

Name _____

Interviews

Work with a partner to act out an interview with the main character in the diary. One partner will pretend to be the character from the diary as an adult. The other partner is the interviewer who is asking the character to reminisce about her childhood.

Preparation

- Read the epilogue in the diary to remember what happened to the character after the diary ended.

- Brainstorm a list of questions to ask the character, some about the time before the diary, some about the time period covered in the diary, and some about her later life. (Remember that some of the questions should be answered with information from the diary, but other questions could draw on things you learned about the period in your research, or could just ask for personal responses. You might even want to throw in a surprise question or two!)

- Choose ten of your best questions and check to make sure you are asking them in a logical order.

- Work together to prepare the answers for the questions.

- Find some appropriate costumes if you wish, and practice the interview with your partner. Try as much as possible not to read from your script.

Presentation

- The interviewer introduces her/himself and welcomes the character being interviewed.

- Present the questions and answers you created and rehearsed.

- At the end of the interview, thank the character.

After listening to several interviews, discuss how others interpreted the character. Did they create different kinds of people? If everyone was using the same information in the diary as their starting point, why did different versions of the character appear in the interviews? Did they ask different kinds of questions?

Memory Boxes

Point out that the characters had life-changing experiences over the course of the diaries. The memory boxes that your students create for the characters should reflect the important events recorded in the diary, and also the historical time period in which the diary was set.

Procedure

— Review the diary and list the things the main character did and enjoyed. For each entry, brainstorm an artifact to represent it in the memory box.

Example

Victoria likes:	Possible artifacts:
poetry	a copy of one of the Robert Louis Stevenson poems she reads; a poem she has written

— Brainstorm other kinds of artifacts that might be appropriate: recipes, drawings of favourite locations in the diary, maps, fabric from favourite clothing, objects from games characters played, copy of music, crafts, favourite books, dried flowers or berries, leaves.

— Create the memory boxes with shoe boxes that students have brought to class. Decorate them with craft paper and designs appropriate for the character (example: ivy design for Ivy Weatherall).

— Set out many different materials for students to use to create artifacts for the memory boxes — construction paper, paints, markers, spools, feathers, yarn, lace, fabric, pieces of leather. Challenge students to "age" the paper they will use for written artifacts.

— Put students into small groups to share their memory boxes and explain why they included different artifacts.

Acknowledgments

Grateful acknowledgment is made for permission to reprint the following:

Page 9: National Gallery of Scotland, Robert Herdman, *Evening Thoughts*, detail, NG 2136.

Pages 11, 12, 13 and 14: National Archives of Canada, J.E. Laughlin, *Crossing the Stream, Ontario — Loyalist Pioneers*, C13992; unknown artist, *Canadian Log-House*, C6753; J.E. Laughlin, *Wood Ashes for Potash Making*, C2197; J.E. Laughlin, *Domestic Spinning and Weaving*, C2481.

Page 15: Map by Paul Heersink/Paperglyphs. Map data © 2000 Government of Canada with permission from Natural Resources Canada.

Page 17: National Gallery of Scotland, Alexander Ignatius Roche, *Nell*, detail, NG 1733.

Page 19: Hudson's Bay Company Archives, Provincial Archives of Manitoba, Samuel Hearne, *York Factory*, HBCA P-112 (N5297).

Page 20: National Archives of Canada, Peter Rindisbacher, C1926.

Page 21: Provincial Archives of Manitoba, E. J. Hutchins, *Old Fort Douglas Red River 1816*, N10113.

Page 26: W. J. Topley/National Archives of Canada, detail, PA151708.

Page 28: National Archives of Canada, PA41785.

Page 29 and 32: Peterborough Archives, detail of *Views/photos taken b/f 1900*, and *Girls leaving Hazel Brae Peterborough, ON 1890s–1900*.

Page 35: Glenbow Archives, Calgary, Canada, detail from Sheffield Family photo, NA 105–5.

Pages 37, 38, 39, 41 and 42: Saskatchewan Archives Board, *Joe Beauchamp store — Qu'Appelle, Sask. 1920's*, R-A7216; *J. Fockler barn with horses — Broadview, Sask. 1928*, R-A18920; *Children in front of Edgewood School — class of 1930–31*, R-A23844; *Homesteaders Peter and Edith Reimer & their children circa 1925*, R-A17267; and *Boys swimming in a slew (or dugout)* date unknown, R-B8270.

National Library of Canada Cataloguing in Publication

Von Heyking, Amy J. (Amy Jeanette), 1965–

   Teaching with Dear Canada books / Amy von Heyking.

Includes bibliographical references.
ISBN 0-7791-1385-3

1. Children's stories, Canadian (English)--Study and teaching (Elementary) 2. Canada--History--Study and teaching (Elementary) 3. Social sciences--Study and teaching (Elementary)--Canada. 4. English language--Study and teaching (Elementary) 5. Language arts (Elementary) I. Title.

PS8039.F5V65 2002   C813'.54   C2002-901144-2
PR9182.2.V65 2002

6 5 4 3 2 1   Printed in Canada   02 03 04 05 06